BUBBER
GOES TO HEAVEN

BUBBER
GOES TO HEAVEN

ARNA BONTEMPS

ILLUSTRATIONS BY

DANIEL MINTER

Introduction by Jim Haskins

Afterword by Charles L. James

OXFORD UNIVERSITY PRESS

New York • Oxford

Oxford University Press

Oxford   New York
Athens Auckland Bangkok Bogotá Bombay
Buenos Aires Calcutta Cape Town Dar es Salaam Delhi
Florence Hong Kong Istanbul Karachi Kuala Lumpur
Madras Madrid Melbourne Mexico City Nairobi
Paris Singapore Taipei Tokyo Toronto Warsaw

and associated companies in

Berlin   Ibadan

Design: Nora C. Wertz

Library of Congress Cataloging-in Publication Data
Bontemps, Arna Wendell, 1902–1973
    Bubber goes to Heaven / Arna Bontemps : illustrations by Daniel
Minter : introduction by Jim Haskins : afterword by Charles L. James
    p. cm. —
    ISBN 0-19-512365-4
    [1. Heaven—Fiction. 2. Angels—Fiction. 3. Dreams—Fiction.
    4. Afro-Americans—Fiction.] I. Minter, Daniel, ill. II. Title.
    PZ7.B6443Bu 1989   98-35830
    [Fic]—dc21   CIP
    AC

1 3 5 7 9 8 6 4 2

Printed in the United States of America on acid-free paper

CONTENTS

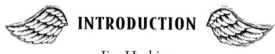

INTRODUCTION

Jim Haskins

Ten-year old Bubber, out coon hunting with his Uncle Demus and friends, climbs up a tall tree called Nebuchadnezzar to flush out their raccoon prey. But the high branch breaks, and both Bubber and the coon go crashing to the ground. Bubber awakes to find that the strong arms lifting him from the ground are not his uncle's, but those of two angels, who have come to take him to heaven.

Heaven looks very much like earth, Bubber decides, except that everyone there wears long nightgowns and has wings. Food is free, and there is plenty of work for all. Bubber is taken in by an angel named Sister Esther, joins the Sunday School choir, and participates in a multicultural children's day program. Learning to fly with his new wings, however, proves difficult.

This previously unpublished children's book by Arna Bontemps, originally entitled *Bubber Joins the Band,* displays the hallmarks of Bontemps's best writing for children—the Deep South locale, biblical references, lyrical tone, gentle humor, realistic rendering of southern black dialect, and emphasis on the world's rainbow of people. Written in the early 1930s, it reveals Bontemps's efforts to learn his craft, to experiment, to gain an audience. It is surprisingly fresh— a testament to the talent of this writer who remains today, as he was in his own time, undeservedly obscure.

Arna Bontemps was born in Alexandria, Louisiana, on October 13, 1902, the descendant of free people of color. His father was a brick mason, and his mother was a teacher. In 1906 the elder Bontemps moved the family to California, where Arna grew up in Los Angeles. The family converted to Seventh-Day Adventism and Arna's father later became a lay minister. His father was disdainful of many blacks, but Arna was curious about his heritage and frustrated in his attempts to find out about his own history from schoolbooks.

On graduation from the small Adventist Pacific Union College, Bontemps moved to New York City to teach at Harlem Academy, a new Adventist school. The Harlem Renaissance was just getting underway, and Bontemps was caught up in the heady creative atmosphere. Having grown up with the Adventist hostility to imaginative writing, Bontemps delighted in the company of other young literary men, such as Langston Hughes, Wallace Thurman, and Countee Cullen. He read voraciously, talked literature constantly, and composed poetry with a sense of freedom he had not enjoyed before. He declared, "We were heralds of a dawning day."

Bontemps had a particular affinity for poetry and submitted his work for the increasing number of poetry prizes available to young black writers. In 1926 and 1927, he twice won the poetry prize offered by *Opportunity: A Journal of Negro Life,* the organ of the National Urban League, and also won the poetry prize of *Crisis,* published by the National Association for the Advancement of Colored People.

By the early 1930s, Bontemps had tried other writing forms, publishing a novel and creating many of the short stories that were published posthumously in 1973. In later years, he also turned his attention to black history and produced several scholarly books. Alone, or with collaborators, he edited anthologies of poetry and folklore. Although much of his work was critically well received, fame and financial success at his craft largely eluded him. For most of his adult life, he worked continuously as a teacher, librarian, and visiting professor to support his wife, Alberta, and six children.

Bontemps was persuaded to try writing for children when his friend Langston Hughes asked him to help rewrite *Popo and Fifina* (1932), a story about Haitian children. It is possible that *Bubber Joins the Band,* which was written in 1932 or 1933, was Bontemps's first solo writing effort for children; whether or not he ever tried to find a publisher for it is not known. Bontemps's first published children's story, *You Can't Pet a Possum,* was issued in 1934. Altogether, Bontemps published some 15 children's books, including biographies of Frederick Douglass, Booker T. Washington, and George Washington Carver, a collective biography on *Famous Negro Athletes,* a book about the Fisk Jubilee Singers, and an anthology of poetry for young people. His children's work also includes several other fiction works, including a second collaboration with Hughes—*The Pasteboard Bandit* (unpublished for 57 years, until 1992)—and three collaborations with the writer Jack Conroy, with whom he also wrote a highly acclaimed study of black migration. He was sole author of *Sad-Faced Boy* (1937) and of *Lonesome Boy* (1955), which is recognized as a literary classic. Its protagonist, a boy who passionately loves his trumpet and follows it wherever it takes him, is also named Bubber—perhaps the same Bubber whose trip-to-heaven story has finally been published nearly 70 years after its creation.

A NOTE FROM THE ARTIST

Daniel Minter

When I first read the manuscript of *Bubber Goes to Heaven,* I was taken in by the warm, down-home voice of the story. It spoke to me of a certain time and place, and I was reminded of my own youth in rural Georgia and the adults who surrounded me there. I grew up in a world similar to Bubber's. Reading the manuscript, I felt like I had traveled back home. Things don't change quickly in the South. Even though the story was written in the 1930s, I recognized the characters and understood their language. Those were people from my family, my church, and my hometown.

Though it was the story that originally attracted me to *Bubber Goes to Heaven,* I became increasingly fascinated with Bontemps's characters, who are all black stereotypes, stylized characters. Bontemps uses black language, and he does so for a reason. For a long time, black people have suffered under negative stereotypes. Blackness was—and still is—seen as threatening and despicable. By taking those black stereotypes and using them to tell a positive story about a loving, hard-working, and deeply religious black community, Bontemps makes an effort to reclaim them.

More than 50 years after Bontemps wrote this story, I am trying to put images to his words in a manner that remains true to his time and relevant to the child of tomorrow. I tried to achieve this by creating artwork that illustrates the surface meaning and events of the story but also hints at the deeper meanings of those events: the magic in the ritual of men teaching boys and the respect and reverence that children give to elders. I thought it most important to show young readers that even though Bubber was taken to a strange place, the things that he took with him were his community and his culture, and that was what made Bubber's adventure a positive one.

Like Bontemps, I consciously exaggerate the "blackness" of my characters. Carved from linoleum blocks, the faces feature large slanted eyes, wide noses, and big lips and are printed in black ink. If someone told you your black skin color and facial features made you a despicable person, you wouldn't want to see or use them in literature or art. You would want to erase them. I try to do the opposite. What I try to do is take those very features that we have been told are shameful and embrace them. I want to celebrate the features of black people. Like Bontemps, I want to take possession of those negative stereotypes by displaying them to the fullest in my art.

Arna Bontemps created a timeless, universal portrait of African-American life, and I hope that I have done the same through my art.

THE COON HUNT

The dogs were running and howling, and the men were right behind them. But Bubber, though he ran as fast as he could, was not able to keep up with the rest. He enjoyed hunting as well as anybody, but when the dogs "jumped a coon," as Uncle Demus said it, there was always such a mad rush that Bubber usually found himself straggling along behind. That was how they had left him this time. The dogs jumped a big brown fellow on the edge of a cornfield and he was giving them a good chase across a meadow.

Bubber could see almost as well as if it were day. There was a big orange moon hanging in a pine tree on a hill, and the clear sky was sprinkled with more stars than he could count. He saw the old coon making for the trees on the side of the hill. The two yellow dogs were right behind. After them came the men, Uncle Demus, Zeke, Tom, and King. On they went, faster and faster.

The men were making almost as much noise as the dogs. Uncle Demus kept calling to his dog, "Get him, Bulger! Get him, boy!" Zeke whistled. Tom howled in a high-pitched voice. King bellowed, his voice rising like a lion's roar.

Bubber's legs were getting tired, but he did not slow down. The coon was coming nearer and nearer to the edge of the pine woods on the side of the hill, and Bubber wanted to be as close as possible when the animal climbed a tree. It would be Bubber's job to follow him up with a stick and shake the coon down from the branches. The dogs would be waiting; they would catch the old fellow as he hit the ground.

14

The wood was familiar to Bubber. It was just an ocean of dark green trees almost all of which looked alike. Three of them, however, were larger than the rest. Two of these stood side by side and were called Adam and Eve. The other, which was even taller, was just at the edge of the woods and was known as Nebuchadnezzar. These three were powerfully big trees, and Bubber hoped the coon would choose a smaller one, but he could climb them if necessary. He could climb any tree in the woods, even if he was just ten and no taller than some little black boys at eight.

Suddenly the coon leaped into the shadows of the trees, and Bubber lost sight of him. The dogs followed, then the men. And when Bubber reached the woods, they were all standing at the trunk of old Nebuchadnezzar and looking up eagerly into its high branches.

"Here is where you come in, Bubber," Uncle Demus called. "Here is yo' job, son."

"Yes, suh," Bubber said, breathing hard. "Just give

15

me a boost up to that first branch, and I'll go up and get him."

"Take this," Zeke said, putting a stick in Bubber's hand. "You might have to give him a punch."

The men hoisted Bubber as high as they could reach. When he got his hands on the first boughs, he found it very easy to climb old Nebuchadnezzar. There were many branches, and he pulled himself from one to the other with ease.

He could hear the coon away up in the top of the tree, and he could hear the dogs barking and the men calling down on the ground. And he could see that he was already above the tops of the smaller trees. He kept climbing, however, getting nearer and nearer to the top.

The moon made the top of the tree bright, and Bubber could see the old coon creeping out on one of the highest branches. Below all was dark. When Bubber looked down, he could see only blackness.

A moment later he reached the branch where the

coon was hanging and said, "Well, Mistah coon, I feel lak yo' time ain't long, suh."

The coon crept farther away, farther out toward the end of the branch. And Bubber began thinking that the dogs wouldn't have much fun with this coon, for the creature would be dead before they got their teeth in him. A fall from this high branch would kill almost anything. The dogs would be disappointed and so would the men, but there was nothing for Bubber to do but climb out and push the old fellow off his perch.

He took the stick firmly in his right hand, got on the limb with the coon and began inching his way out. Easily, slowly, bit by bit he moved. The coon whined. Then Bubber felt the tree sway, heard a cracking sound, and knew that the limb had broken with him and the coon. In the next instant he felt himself plunging downward, and everything got blacker than midnight.

The next thing he knew he was being lifted up by strong arms. At first Bubber could not talk, but after a short while he said, "Dat you, Uncle Demus? Dat you, Zeke and King?"

And a voice answered, "Nah, we ain't your Uncle Demus, and we ain't Zeke and King. We is God's big angels, and we's taking you to heaven, Bubber."

WHERE EVERY DAY
IS SUNDAY

During most of the journey Bubber was afraid and kept his eyes closed. But finally one of the angels said, "I think we've carried this chile far enough. He oughta could walk the rest of the way."

And the other one answered, "Well I say as much." Then he shook Bubber. "Open your eyes, suh. What in the nation is you trying to do—play possum? Get down and walk some."

Bubber blinked and opened his eyes as his feet

touched the ground, but the sun was so bright he couldn't see much at first. He walked behind the angels without complaining, however, and after a while everything became clear. The angels, he saw, were big tall men like his Uncle Demus and Zeke and Tom. They had powerful wings on their backs, and they wore nightgowns instead of clothes. In fact, they looked just like any angels are supposed to look, and Bubber felt mighty proud to be walking behind them.

The fields were green and quiet on the side of the road, but Bubber was surprised and frightened when he saw a huge lion lying in the grass. But the animal only wagged his tail and whinneyed when the three passed, so Bubber supposed he must have been a tame circus lion.

As he walked, Bubber felt little pains on his shoulder blades. He kept reaching his hands behind his back and rubbing the sore spots, and he wondered what caused the peculiar hurting. He was not at all tired, and he couldn't see how walking would give him pains so high on his back anyhow. It might have come from that fall from the pine tree, but it didn't seem like that kind of hurting. Bubber wanted to speak to the angels about it, but they were so busy laughing and talking between themselves he decided not to bother them.

They reached the top of a hill and Bubber saw just ahead the chimneys and roofs of a town. Around it there was a high wall like a whitewashed fence taller than a grown man could see over. Where the road entered town there was a big gate made of cross strips, and there were horses and mules and wagons of all kinds tied to the hitching bars just outside. An old gray-haired man with a black evening coat and bright tan shoes sat in a chair tilted against the wall and kept the gate. He wore a pair of spectacles that slid down almost to the end of his nose, and at the moment of Bubber's arrival he was smoking his corncob pipe and reading a newspaper.

"Evening," the old fellow said as the angels approached him.

"Evening, Peter," one of the angels said. "What's the news?"

"Nothing much. I just see where the ladies' club is gonna have a church supper next week for the benefit of the orphan angels. Who you got there?"

"This boy is named Bubber, I b'lieve."

"Yes, suh, that's it," Bubber spoke up.

"Well dog my cats," said the old man. "I b'lieve he's a smart young-un, too."

"He'll do," an angel answered. "He's kinda little and puny though."

Bubber looked again at the long line of wagons, carts, horses, and mules.

"What is all these here rigs doing out here?" he asked old Peter politely.

"Church, chile. Them b'longs to folks what came up to church."

"Church? This ain't Sunday, is it?"

The old gatekeeper took his pipe in his left hand and smiled kindly.

"Every day is Sunday up here, Bubber," he said. "Didn't you learn that in Sunday School?"

"Oh, yes, suh," Bubber said quickly. "I 'bout forgot."

Old Peter laughed aloud and put his hand on Bubber's shoulder.

"Well, be good, son. Don't run wid no bad boys."

"A'right, suh," Bubber said, closing the gate behind him.

Inside the big gate the angels who had brought Bubber to heaven left him to get along by himself in that strange town. They were hot and perspiring from the journey, and they left Bubber at the first street corner.

"You'll be all right," one of them said. "You'll meet up with some good people befo' long. They'll take care of you."

Bubber felt disappointed. He did not like being left alone like this, and he was a bit frightened. But he did not forget his manners.

"Thank y'all angels for bringing me, just the same," he said timidly.

The angels were already walking away.

"Oh, you welcome," one of them called over his shoulder.

There were many people in the streets of the town, and Bubber noticed that all of them turned around and looked at him when he passed. Some youngsters, playing on the curb, put their hands in front of their faces and snickered. But Bubber did not know why. He only knew that he felt very strange and lonesome in this town and that his shoulders were hurting again, hurting worse than ever.

At a street corner in front of a drugstore Bubber stopped to rub his back against a telephone pole; and while he stood there, the pain became so sharp that he could not keep from crying. Tears ran down his face. Rubbing the sore shoulders did help them a little, but this was surely the worst misery Bubber had ever suffered. It was so bad, in fact, that Bubber did not notice the crowd of people who gathered around him until a fat lady angel stepped up and put her arm around him. Her head was tied in a red bandanna, and except for her wings and nightgown she would have resembled very closely the large black woman whose picture Bubber had seen on boxes of pancake flour. But she was kind and smiled as she spoke.

"What the trouble, son?"

"My back," Bubber murmured. "My back hurts."

She put her hand inside his jacket and passed it gently across his shoulder blades.

"Um hunh," she said. "Just what I thought. Yo' wings is beginning to sprout. Don't cry. It'll be over soon."

"Wings!" Bubber exclaimed.

"That's all. Just growing pains," she said. "Come 'long with me. I'll take you home and put some Vaseline on them."

Bubber put his hand in the angel's and followed her gladly. He was already beginning to feel much better.

28

TEN LITTLE ANGELS
IN A BAND

One little, two little, three little angels,
Four little, five little, six little angels,
Seven little, eight little, nine little angels
Ten little angels in a band—

Bubber heard the singing from the window of his tiny attic room, but he did not know where it came from or who was doing it. The singing was beautiful just the same, and Bubber jumped out of bed and went to the window to hear more. The voices were accompanied by stringed instruments that sounded somewhat like guitars and mandolins, and the group did not stop singing and playing till they had counted to one hundred little angels in a band.

When they were finished, Bubber clapped his hands out of the window and called out loudly, "Sing some mo', you-all. Sing some mo'."

There was no answer. After a while the large lady angel who had taken Bubber home came upstairs quietly. She stood in the door frame with her hands on her hips and watched Bubber as he leaned out of the window and called to the singers. He had not heard her footsteps; and when he turned and saw her there, he was surprised and a trifle frightened.

"Well I declare," she said. "What you mean by making all this fuss before breakfast? You'll wake up the whole neighborhood."

"I didn't go to do it," Bubber said, astonished. "Sho nuff, Sister Esther, I was just clapping for that purty song."

"Well," she said, "mind out how you holler. Plenty folks ain't up yet." A little later she added, "Does you like singing and playing, Bubber?"

"Yes'm," Bubber said eagerly. "I sho do."

"Well maybe you can join the band after you been round here a little longer. That was the Sunday School choir you heard. They's practicing up for the children's day program."

"Oh," Bubber was too excited to say more. He could feel his heart thumping. This was going to be a fine place to live after all.

"Put on your clothes," Sister Esther said. "Soon's I get this room cleaned and the bed made we can have breakfast. After that we can go to church."

Bubber was still wearing the pair of patched pants and the little red jacket in which he had gone coon hunting. While he was putting them on, Sister Esther took the cover off the bed and hung it out the window to sun. Then they went down to the kitchen and had a breakfast of pancakes, molasses, and golden scrambled eggs.

Later the church bell rang, and Bubber and Sister Esther went out together. They walked hand in hand to the church around the corner, and the big lady angel led Bubber to a seat in the Sunday School room.

"You stay here till time for preaching," she said. "I'll come back and get you then—hear?"

"Yes'm," Bubber said timidly.

"Now don't run round with the rest of these young-uns and get lost."

"No'm, Sister Esther," he said.

Many other youngsters came in and filled

the seats in the room. They were much like the children who attended the Shiloh Sunday School down in Huntsville, but Bubber was the only one who did not wear a clean white nightgown instead of clothes. And of course he felt very strange and embarrassed in his ragged pants and jacket.

The leader of the meeting was a young woman. She came to Bubber and asked his name before she took her seat at the front. Then she tapped a small bell and everything became quiet. A moment later Bubber heard familiar singing voices in the room above, and the children's choir came marching down the stairs.

Each member of the little angel band had a silver harp in his hand and a golden crown on his head, and as they marched and sang their big eyes sparkled. They went into the front rows of chairs, and all sat down together. Then the leader rose and started the meeting.

"We got one little new member with us today," she said. "I want him to stand up so everybody can see him."

Bubber stood. Every head turned toward him.

"Maybe he'll say something," the leader said.

"My name is Bubber, and I wants to join the band. Amen," Bubber said promptly.

"Well ain't that fine? He is named Bubber and he wants to join the band. Let me see. Does you know the books of the Bible?"

"Yes'm," said Bubber. "Genesis, Exodus, Leviticus, Numbers, Deuteronomy—"

"That'll do. That's fine," said the leader, cutting him off. "Now let me hear you say the Commandments."

Bubber said them without a mistake, just as he had learned them back at Shiloh. Then she asked for the Lord's Prayer, the Beatitudes, and the Shepherd Psalm, and Bubber recited each one just as fast as he could say the words.

"I got a bookmark for learning these," Bubber said modestly when he had finished.

"A bookmark! Well why didn't you tell me that?"

the leader exclaimed. "All the children what got them long purple book marks at Shiloh can join without reciting. We's glad to have you in our Sunday School, Bubber, and we'll see that you get your robe before next week. I'm gonna see Sister Esther 'bout teaching you a piece for children's day, too."

"Thank you, ma'am," Bubber said and sat down.

After saying the Golden Text and studying the lesson, the children were dismissed. Bubber did not go out but waited in his seat for Sister Esther. When all the rest were gone, the choir members went upstairs to leave their harps and crowns.

One little cherub lingered behind. She had big white eyes and shining white teeth, and her hair was tied with white strings in a hundred little wiry twists on her head. As she went up the stairs behind the others, sliding her face along the rail, she called back, "Good-bye, Bubber."

"G'-bye," Bubber said timidly.

Then he snatched his cap from under the chair, ran

to the foot of the stairs, and was about to follow the others up into the choir room, but he saw Sister Esther standing at the door and he changed his mind.

"Um hunh," she said. "Just getting ready to start romping up and down them stairs. You come on to church with me, suh, and I don't want no fidgeting whilst the preacher is preaching—hear?"

"Yes'm," Bubber said. "I hears, Sister Esther."

4

SEEING THE TOWN

Bubber's wings were growing well. There was no more pain on his shoulder blades, and he was beginning to feel very much at home in heaven. But he had only seen a small part of the town and he was anxious to take a long walk and become better acquainted with the sights.

He told Sister Esther of his wish, and she said that he might go if he got up early in the morning and helped her with the housecleaning.

That was all the encouragement he needed. Bubber

was up before the sun. He took a bucket of water and a scrub brush and went out to clean the white stone door stoop in front of Sister Esther's house. But he was not the only person on the street scrubbing the stoop in the cool of the morning. All along the street there were lady angels with mop pails and soapy water making the little white stoops shine.

Bubber tried to remember where he had seen little white door stoops like these before. They were familiar all right. Where had he seen them? Then suddenly it came to his mind. It was in Baltimore. He had gone there with Uncle Demus to see old Aunt Clo. They had made the trip with railroad passes that King had secured by working in the train yards. And in that big city the houses had little white door stoops like these.

When his job was done, Bubber poured the soapy scrub water into the street and carried the pail and brush around to Sister Esther in the backyard. She was washing clothes. In the middle of the yard there was a big black kettle in which some white pieces were boiling

over an outdoor fire. Bubber stood beside the washtub a minute before he spoke. Then he said, "You sho has got a big washing, Sister Esther."

"Hm," she smiled, wiping her face with her apron. "All these clothes ain't mine, son. I takes in a little washing so as to make some spending money. Most folks up here don't like to wash their own clothes, but just the same they likes to put on clean things every day; so I have more washing than I can do all the time. That's one of the things what makes heaven so good. There ain't never no hard times here."

It was no wonder, Bubber thought, that people tried so hard to make heaven their home. Even the washerwomen had plenty of work and nothing to worry about. It was wonderful, and the thought made him more eager than ever to wander about town and see things.

"I'm ready to go now," he told Sister Esther. "I done scrubbed them steps so bright you can see your face in them."

"Well, all right," she said. "Whilst you's walking around, though, I want you to take this quarter and buy me two yards of white flannel to make you a robe for Sunday."

She put the coin in Bubber's hand, and he clasped his fingers tightly around it.

"Yes'm," he said, skipping through the backyard gate. "I'll get it for you, Sister Esther."

The business section of the town was only a few blocks away, and Bubber found that there the streets were filled with wagons and carts even at this early hour. Most of the carts were loaded with fruit and green vegetables. They were driven by country angels covered with dust from their long drive.

All of these wagons and carts were going to the square in the heart of town. There Bubber saw, sitting on a green knoll and surrounded by oak trees, a large white brick building like the courthouse in Huntsville. In the streets that ran around the square, there was a great jostle of vehicles and people. Many of the angels had already arranged their fruit and vegetables in attractive pyramids and blocks and hills.

Bubber walked in and out among the tempting piles of fruit and wished for an orange or an apple. But he had no money except for the quarter Sister Esther had given him for white flannel; so he could only look and wish. After a while, however, an old man noticed the look on Bubber's face and said, "Does you want some of this here fruit, son?"

"Well, I does and I doesn't," Bubber said promptly.

The old man rolled his eyes playfully. "Now what in the name of sense do that signify—you does and you doesn't?"

Bubber dropped his eyes. He was a little ashamed. "I went to say I wants some oranges mighty bad, but I ain't got no money to buy none with."

The old country angel laughed out very loudly, slapping his knee with his hand. He paused, then laughed some more. And Bubber was so embarrassed, he could hardly stand still.

"Well I oughta knowed you ain't been here long," the old fellow said finally. "But these ain't to sell, son. Everything to eat is free in heaven. If you see anything you want, just help yourself, see?"

"Oh, I understand," Bubber said. "Thank you, suh."

And without waiting a moment he filled his pockets and the inside of his jacket with the biggest oranges he saw. A little later he went into a store and helped himself to stick candy, chocolate bars, and soda pop. In a bakery he selected doughnuts and apple pie. Then, his arms full, he sat down on a curbstone and began eating. And for the first time, heaven really seemed like heaven to Bubber.

WHITE FLANNEL

When his stomach was full, Bubber began to feel sleepy. He had not eaten all the fruit and sweets in his pockets and jacket and arms, but he decided he would have to save the rest till some time later. So he looked about for a shady place to lie down and take a nap.

The only trees in sight were those on the square, in the courthouse yard. Bubber made up his mind to stretch out on the grass beneath one of them. So he crossed the street, slipped between the rails of the

wrought-iron fence, and sat down at the foot of a
statue of Abraham Lincoln. His
pockets and the inside of
his jacket were still so
tightly stuffed with
food that he could
not lie down
without crush-
ing something.
So he emptied
them slowly and
made a neat pile of
oranges, doughnuts,
and candy on the
grass. Then he leaned

back, his head touching the bottom of the statue, and fell asleep.

A short while later, only a few moments it seemed, Bubber felt a hand on his shoulder shaking him and heard somebody say, "Wake up there, boy! What you doing sleeping in here? Don't you know where you is?"

Bubber opened his eyes with a start. He was trembling as he gathered up his little pile of goodies and rose to his feet. Then for the first time he got a good look at the big blue-robed angel who had awakened him. The fellow wore a policeman's cap and had a large policeman's badge pinned to his robe; in his hand there was a policeman's stick, and a policeman's pistol was hanging in a holster at his side. Bubber quaked with fear as the huge policeman angel looked down on him.

"No, suh," he said. "I doesn't know where I is, but I reckon I ain't supposed to be here just the same."

"Nah, you ain't," the angel said. "The Lawd's office and his courtroom is in this building. This the place where the books is kept, too. No chillun is allowed to play round here, and we don't let *nobody* get on this grass. See?"

"Yes, suh," Bubber said, slipping through the fence. "I know just what you mean, and you ain't got to tell me two times. You means 'git !' and I'm done gone."

It was plain that Bubber had slept longer than he realized at first, for the sun was high now and moving toward the west. Bubber knew that it was time he started home. The angels with the carts and wagons were sitting on boxes now, nodding in the afternoon sun, and the heaps of fruit and vegetables were much smaller than they had been earlier in the day. The mules were restless at the hitching bars; they kept pawing at the cobblestones with their feet and switching at flies with their tails.

Suddenly Bubber remembered the quarter in his hand. What was it for? Sister Esther had asked him to buy something, what was it? Cloth? That was it, some cloth to make Bubber a robe. He walked half a block to the dry goods store and went inside.

"Something for you?" a young woman asked.

"Yes'm," Bubber said, dropping his quarter on the counter. "Give me two yards of blue flannel."

With the package under his arm, Bubber started home. A block from the doorstep he recognized a familiar old man standing on the sidewalk with a fishing pole over his shoulder and a string of fish in his hand. He was talking to Sister Esther and holding the string of fish up for her to see. Bubber could see that the old man was Peter, the gatekeeper, so he hurried down the block to get there before the man left. When he reached the spot, he heard Sister Esther saying, "Peter, you sho do love to fish."

"Yes," the old man told her. "I loves to fish more'n I love to eat. Fishing used to be my trade. But they keeps me so busy at the gate up here, I don't get much chance to go to the river." Then he noticed Bubber standing beside Sister Esther. "Well will you look at this boy's wings. How they is growing! He just came here the other day."

Sister Esther smiled and patted Bubber's head. "They is growing in nicely, thanks," she said. "I just sent him for some flannel to make him his first robe." She turned to Bubber. "Did you get it, son?"

"Yes'm," Bubber said, handing her the package. "Two yards."

Sister Esther opened the package. A look of disgust came over her face. Peter could see that something was wrong.

"What's the matter, Esther?" he asked.

"I told that boy to get me white flannel and he done brought blue!"

Bubber's heart sank. "I forgot," he said. "I forgot you said white, Sister Esther."

"What's all that in your pockets and in your jacket?" Bubber started taking the good things out and putting them in Sister Esther's hand. "So this is how come you couldn't remember what I told you, hunh? Well, just give it all to me. And I want you to go straight back to the dry goods store and change this flannel. You

51

better hurry too—else I'll make you stay home from
Sunday School."

"Yes, that's right," said Peter. "You hurry back,
son, because I'm gonna leave two of these red snappers
here for you and Sister Esther. Besides I want to see you
wearing that new robe by children's day."

"Yes, suh," Bubber said politely, but tears were in
his eyes as he trotted down the shining street to the dry
goods store.

CHILDREN'S DAY

When children's day came, Bubber wore the new flannel nightgown to church, but he exchanged it for another costume before the program started.

All the youngsters met in the choir room upstairs. There they removed their white robes and put on clothes that represented the dress of people from all parts of the earth and from all periods of time. It was a big job to dress so many fidgety youngsters, and the Sunday School leader was kept very busy, and Bubber had to wait a long time for his turn.

When finally she did reach him, she put on Bubber a little brown Indian suit trimmed with red. Then she gave him a headpiece with many bright feathers in it and handed him a bow and arrow. And Bubber, who had always wanted an Indian outfit, felt so proud his chest nearly popped.

The other children swarmed and buzzed in the room like bees. Some of the little girls wore long black dresses with bonnets to match; some wore spotted things that looked like leopard skins. And Bubber noticed that the child who had spoken to him on the stair the first day he went to Sunday School in heaven was one of them. Her hair was still tied in little tight twists, but what she now wore was a leopard skin tied around her waist. She carried a little pasteboard spear in her hand. When she saw Bubber standing as straight as a plank, with his head back and his chest pushed out, she smiled sweetly and rolled her eyes in admiration. And Bubber knew then that he was the most dressed-up little angel in the place.

After a while a little bell rang and everything became quiet in the room. Then the leader said, "Now we is 'bout ready to begin. Y'all cherubs get in line—hear?"

"Yes'm," the children said and began at once to find their places.

The leader peeped through a crack into the big church room.

"The church is just packed," she said. "You is all got to shine tonight. You must talk loud; and don't forget your pieces." She paused a moment. "You can go out now. Remember to walk slow, and don't push and pull when you get on the platform."

The row started down the stairs, and Bubber felt his heart pounding like a hammer. He was terribly afraid to walk out before that large crowd of people. But there was one thing he did not have to worry about: he knew his piece well. He remembered every word of it. He could almost say it in his sleep. And he had practiced saying it very loud, too. He only wished he were not so frightened now and that his knees

would stop knocking together.

They marched through the Sunday School room and into the main auditorium where the line formed a half circle on the platform. Bubber was the last to enter the room, and there was hardly room for him to stand. He was crowded against a large potted plant the leaves of which brushed his face and annoyed him greatly. But he felt that he could stand that if he could only stop trembling.

Suddenly the first child stepped forward. He was a small boy dressed in furs that covered him from head to foot, except for the front of his face. Another large white fur he carried on his arm. He bowed as he reached the center of the stage and began reciting.

> *From Greenland's icy mountains*
> *I come with you to dwell,*
> *I want to learn the living way*
> *And hear the tales you tell.*
>
> *My home was in the frozen north*
> *In a cave of ice and snow,*

But I have come to Canaan land
Where summer flowers blow.

There isn't much in that far land
Of which to tell or sing,
But this white fur of the polar bear
As a thankful gift I bring.

He placed the fur on an altar in front of the platform, bowed again, then returned to his place.

The second child was a little girl. She wore a pair
of pajama pants and a long jacket, and there was an arti-
ficial pigtail hanging down her back. She held in her
hand a pair of chopsticks and a bowl of rice. She
walked to the center of the stage.

I am a little Chinese girl—
'A-ha' for shame they say—
My parents wished I were a boy
And cast my soul away.

But I have reached the blissful land
Of everlasting day,

And on the altar with your fur
My humble gift I lay.

She went back to her place, and Bubber heard a murmur of approval pass over the big audience. He saw old Brother Peter, standing by the door with an usher's badge on his coat, wipe a tear from his eye.

Next there followed a child from India. Then one from Arabia, and then a little pilgrim child spoke. Bubber lost track of them and their gifts. He began saying his own piece in his mind, getting ready for his turn when it should come. He paid attention to nothing else till he saw the little girl with the leopard skin step forward.

I am a little Zulu girl.
Faraway was my home.
I dwelt in lovely Africa,
And with my gift I come.

I lay upon the altar here
My dreaded spear so bright,
For I'll not kill and I'll not wound
Before His holy sight.

That sounded very good to Bubber; and before he knew it, he blurted out, "Amen!"

"Listen to that boy say 'Amen,'" cried Brother Peter in the back of the room. "I b'lieve he gonna make a preacher. I sho do."

Everyone laughed softly. Then when it was over the speeches continued. Finally Bubber's turn came.

> *My home was a wigwam by a stream*
> *In a land both wild and far,*
> *Where hostile tribes swept down at night*
> *With implements of war.*
>
> *My father was an Indian brave,*
> *My mother planted maize,*
> *I was their first and only son——*

Suddenly Bubber came to a stop. His mouth was empty of words. He could not recall the next line of his piece. All the cherubs looked at him, rolled their eyes, and giggled. The people in the audience began to whisper, and Brother Peter got up nervously and began walking up and down the aisle with his hands behind him. The leader of the Sunday School tried to whisper the next word to Bubber, but he could not hear what she said. Bubber was just ready to cry when Sister Esther rose in the back part of the room and called out, "He through, Brother Peter. Bubber ain't got no mo' to say. He done said his piece."

Bubber understood that. She meant for him to bow and pretend that he had said all, to make people think he had not forgotten. So he made a big fine bow and turned to go to his place in the line. But there was something else he had forgotten. He still held the bow and arrow in his hands. He had to leave them on the altar. Bubber was miserable again and terribly puzzled.

He turned around, rushed back to the center of the platform and dropped the gift on the altar.

"Here mine," he said loudly. "I 'bout forgot to leave it."

The people in the church were laughing heartily when Bubber reached his place in the line, and the other youngsters were giggling as if their sides would split. Bubber could feel cool perspiration on his forehead. In the midst of the commotion he heard the Sunday School leader saying,

"Go on, Bubber; you lead the line out."

They marched into the Sunday School room, and all the children except Bubber continued upstairs. Bubber was ashamed to go up there to change his clothes. He decided to wait downstairs till the others left the choir room.

While he waited, however, he heard a voice on the stairs; and when he looked up, he saw the little Zulu cherub with her face on the banister, calling down, "Good-night, Bubber. Good-night."

And right away he began to feel better. He began to think that perhaps his speech had not sounded so terrible after all.

"Good-night," Bubber said politely.

He decided to go upstairs and put on his robe.

LEARNING TO FLY

Bubber soon forgot about the poor showing he had made on the children's day program. The other youngsters almost forgot about it, too, for they never mentioned it anymore unless somebody happened to say, "Here mine" or "I 'bout forgot." Then they would laugh and point at Bubber, and one of them would say, "He through, Brother Peter. He ain't got no mo' to say!" And all would laugh together. Most of the time, however, nobody thought of that program.

The thing that was troubling Bubber's mind now

was how he could learn to use his wings. They had grown out big and strong, and the old folks told Sister Esther it was time that boy learned to fly. There was no need for cuddling him. Many children learned to fly when they had been in heaven no longer than Bubber.

Learning to fly was something like learning to swim. It just took nerve and determination. When one lost his fear of high air, the rest was easy. Many children had learned by being thrown off hillsides, some by falling from housetops. But Bubber had not forgotten his fall from the big pine tree, and he preferred learning in the more regular way by flying up from the ground.

Every morning he practiced a little while. He would run along in the street, then suddenly extend his wings and sail a few feet. Occasionally he would give them a few flaps, but he never got very far off the ground. When he felt himself rising, he always lost his nerve and sailed down again. He could not bear the odd feeling of his feet dangling in the air unable to touch the ground.

Sister Esther watched him from the doorsteps. "Keep on going," she would cry. "Keep a-flapping your wings, Bubber."

Bubber would make a few more flaps, then sail down. The other cherubs of the neighborhood would fly up above and call down, "Come on up, Bubber."

Well, Bubber appreciated their encouragement, and he was trying hard, but learning to fly was no easy job—even after you had your wings. Bubber sat down on the curbstone to rest and think. It seemed impossible for him to learn to fly in that way. No matter how he tried, he got no farther than a few feet from the ground.

He would just naturally have to try another method of learning.

The only thing he could think of was to climb up on top of Sister Esther's house and fly down. He shuddered at the thought, but he was now willing to try, if it would help him fly.

He got up from the curb and walked back to the doorstep where Sister Esther stood with a broom and dustpan in her hand.

"I'm gonna get up top the house and fly down." he said. "I been having a hard time down here. Can't get my feet off the ground."

"Well, I say as much," she told him. "Now you talking. You gonna be flying before you know it, too."

Bubber went up the stairs to the attic. Then he climbed out of the tiny window and crept up the roof to the peak of the gable. There he sat down and waited. The little group of cherubs flew overhead and landed on the roof nearby. Sister Esther stuck her head out of the attic window. Bubber stood up, ready to jump. He shut

his eyes and began saying a little piece he knew.

"One for the money,
Two for the show—"

He paused, and Sister Esther called, "Don't forget to flap your wings, Bubber. Jump off and keep a-flapping your wings, son."

One of the little cherubs said, "Yes, that's right, Bubber, don't forget to flap your wings."

Bubber bit his lip and began his piece again.

"One for the money
Two for the show,
Three to make ready
And four to go."

Off he went. He felt himself going through the air fast. Then he felt himself hit the ground very hard. Bubber groaned in pain and turned over on his face.

8

GOOD-BYE, BUBBER

"I forgot to flap my wings," he sobbed. "I forgot to flap my wings."

His face was buried in a pillow. He could not stop crying. Both his legs were hurting terribly. There were people walking around him, and Bubber could hear their voices. One of them said, "What in the name of sense that boy talking 'bout—he forgot to flap his wings."

After a while somebody knelt beside the bed and took Bubber's hand. He heard the familiar voice of

Uncle Demus say, "What the matter, son. Is you hurt bad?"

Bubber opened his eyes and looked about the room. He was back in his own cabin home in Alabama. King and Tom were standing near the door and Aunt Sarah was by the stove, stirring something in a pot.

"I was just trying my wings," Bubber said.

"You was s'posed to been shaking that coon off the limb," King answered.

"I mean in heaven," Bubber said. "I been in heaven."

"Heaven!" Aunt Sarah left her pot. "What that you say?"

"Lawdy," Uncle Demus cried. "Was you having a vision when we picked you up for dead out there underneath that tree?"

"I reckon so," Bubber said. "I seen heaven and the angels and Saint Peter and everybody. I was just learning to fly."

"Well did you see the Lawd?" Aunt Sarah asked eagerly.

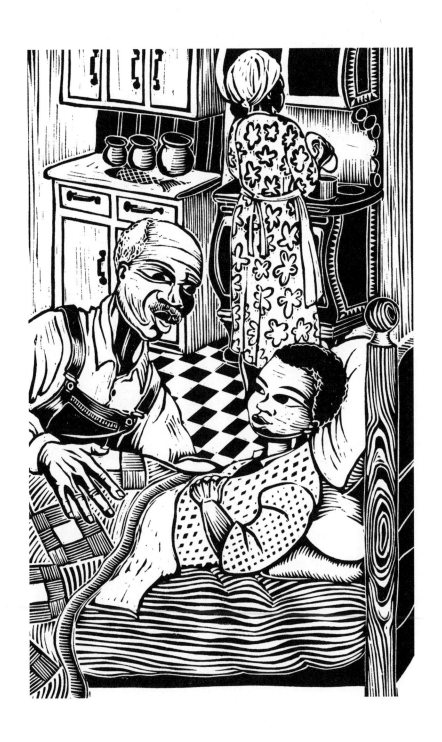

Bubber thought a moment. It *was* funny that he had not seen the Lord in heaven.

"No," he said. "I didn't see the Lawd, but I seen the square and the courthouse."

Aunt Sarah went back to her pot.

"Shucks," she said. "You ain't seen heaven if you ain't seen the Lawd. You ain't had no vision neither. You is just had a nightmare. Lie still now. Them two broken legs of yours might get out of place again if you keep a-twitching like that."

The men went outside, and Bubber lay very still. He was not sure now whether he had been to heaven or not. But he could still hear the youngsters and Sister Esther calling to him and saying, "Keep a-flapping your wings, Bubber." He could still see the little Zulu cherub sliding her face up the banister of the Sunday School stairs and saying, "Good-night, Bubber. Good-night."

 **THE END**

AFTERWORD

By Charles L. James

In a 1965 essay written for *Harper's Magazine* and entitled "Why I Returned," Arna Bontemps proclaimed his love for the Southland. This was not a new love, but it was his first public confession, expressing the potency of his first years in Louisiana before his parents took him to California. Evidently, Bontemps's early childhood shaped his sensibilities and later emerged in the form of his fiction for children in the 1930s. This decade was the most embattled period of his long writing career, but it was Bontemps's most productive period as well, when his commitment to writing for children was established. Given his long love affair with the South, small wonder that his portrayal of Bubber's remarkable adventures in the Alabama countryside reads like the recovery of experiences long lost.

With the possible exception of his first effort at a novel (the autobiographical *Chariot in the Clouds,* 1929), *Bubber Goes to Heaven* (originally named *Bubber Joins the Band,* written in the early 1930s) is Bontemps's most personal fiction. Neither work was published, but they reveal Bontemps's familiarity with black vernacular culture and anticipate by better than two decades the issuance of the landmark *Book of Negro Folklore* (1958), edited with

Langston Hughes, his favorite and most frequent collaborator. Looking at Bontemps's personal journey into the 1930s is one way of understanding Bubber's journey to heaven and his failure to gain full membership there.

Arna Bontemps was born in the Red River region of central Louisiana in 1902. It was the early era of Jim Crow, and the industrious river town of Alexandria and its surroundings can only be described as precarious if not dangerous territory for most African Americans. Arna and his sister, Ruby (born nearly two years later), were members of one of the best known "colored" families in Rapides Parish. Their father was a skilled brick mason and their mother taught in the local colored schools, but it was their maternal grandparents, Sarah and Joseph Pembroke, who had carved out a reputation in this tiny farming community. Grandfather Pembroke had worked as an assistant to a white mortician in Alexandria, and Grandmother Pembroke was famed for her talent as a seamstress.

Vivid memories of his early days in Louisiana left an indelible mark on Bontemps and were chiefly associated with his grandmother, "whose love," he would write years later, "mattered so much." Sarah Pembroke was a remarkable woman, spirited and spiritual and unapologetically opinionated. Semiretired from her seamstress shop, she filled in for Arna's parents, whose work kept them away from home for extended intervals. "My hand was in hers a good part of the time," he reported.

Those were flawless days for the precocious and impressionable child. There was a spacious house boasting two chimneys serving four fireplaces, an indoor kitchen, and an eight-foot-wide central hallway. According to local historians, the Pembroke place was more in keeping with the home of a middle-class white family in rural Louisiana than with a typical black home. There were pecan trees, a white picket fence, and a mare named Daisy that pulled the family buggy about town or across the Red River and deep into the piney woods. All these things made an imprint on young Arna's mind. And then suddenly the idyll ended.

In the spring of 1906, before Jim Crow segregation held any meaning for Arna and his sister, the children traveled with their mother by train to Los Angeles to join their father, who had gone ahead to find work. Later, Arna learned that his father was fed up with the overwhelming racism ("the conditions") in Louisiana and was planning to provide his family with a fresh start. Later still, he learned that his mother and his grandmother were afflicted with tuberculosis and that they hoped to find relief in the drier California climate. In time, most of the Alexandria household found its way to Southern California: the newcomers arrived with their central Louisiana vernacular intact only to discover that their desire to re-create what they left behind added up to little more than nostalgia.

Bontemps's sojourn in California lasted 18 years— through the death of his maternal grandfather; through his parents' conversion to Seventh-Day Adventism shortly after their arrival; and through his profound sorrow over his mother's death when he was 12 years old. The conversion was less memorable than the sorrows, but as was the case for novelist Richard Wright, Adventism profoundly affected Bontemps's writing career, so much that when they met for the first time in Chicago in 1936 and for the last time in Paris in 1961, their conversation turned quickly to the Adventists' ban on fictional narrative and "secular" philosophy. Bontemps reported that Wright's sentiments concerning his early church experiences were unforgiving.

On the other hand, Bontemps described his exposure to Adventism as a "literary deprivation" that "had left a void" in his adolescent years but one that "had not been complete." That is, he claims to have had the good fortune of resources that enabled him to cope with the bitterness Wright felt: his mother's love of poetry (her favorite was Longfellow's "Evangeline"); his Great-uncle Buddy's folktales and ghost stories; and his growing fascination with the essays and "forbidden" fiction of Robert Louis Stevenson.

Arna and his sister had been baptized Catholics in Louisiana. It was their father's denomination. Their mother was Methodist, and her unease with Catholicism and her deep spirituality set the climate for the change to a denomination the family could embrace in their new home. The parents' choice in 1907 of the Adventist church placed them among the earliest black adherents of Adventism in Southern California. Thereafter, their way of life was fixed in accordance with strict Adventist requirements, which included a spare diet and Sabbath observances on Saturdays. Furthermore, Arna's formal education—from elementary school through college—depended largely on Adventist institutions, where more often than not he was the sole black student in his class.

When his mother's illness worsened, Arna's family went to live "in the country" with Grandmother Pembroke, on the outskirts of Los Angeles. There she had been joined by her bachelor brother, Buddy, recently arrived from Louisiana. Arna was enthralled by this unlikely little derelict of a man who smoked a corncob pipe, wore oversized clothes, and spoke unself-consciously in his homey Louisiana language: "Folks talk a lot about California," he often said, "but I'd a heap rather be down home than here, if it wasn't for the conditions."

Arna's father voiced similar sentiments, but the richness and vitality of Great-uncle Buddy's Louisiana commentary animated the southern scenario in a way that his father's accounts had not. Buddy's southern memories revealed a verve that emerged from an expressive folk heritage that Arna's father found embarrassing and demeaning. Arna affectionately recalled, for instance, that Buddy "loved dialect stories, preacher stories, ghost stories, slave and master stories. He half-believed in signs and charms and mumbo jumbo, and he believed wholeheartedly in ghosts." Arna's father, on the other hand, was quick to label Buddy a negative role model, an alcoholic and a wastrel.

Determined to secure a respectable life for his son, Arna's father packed him off to the Adventist academy in the beautiful San Fernando Valley, with the instructions not to "go up there acting colored." To his father's proud satisfaction, Arna excelled at the white academy and continued on at Pacific Union College, an Adventist institution in the Napa Valley. Shy and quiet though he was, young Arna had already been claimed by the mysterious, colorful elements of his southern black background—elements and values embodied by his irrepressible great-uncle.

The spectacular California settings enhanced Arna's love of the outdoors and accentuated his sense of nature's spiritual qualities. "It was a lovely place to be," he reflected. "My [dormitory] window opened on a glen and beyond this charming passage there was the then famous thousand acres of mighty redwoods. At night after lights-out I listened to the sound of the trees." These sites, however, did not resolve in his father's favor the rift between Buddy's folk values and his father's opposing standards. Rather, it is probable that the bucolic settings contributed to Arna's recovery of his childhood idyll in Rapides Parish, Louisiana, now loosely linked with easygoing Buddy.

In addition, summer vacations in Los Angeles brought Arna into close contact with his cultural self through folks like Buddy arriving from the rural South. In his *Harper's* essay, Bontemps wrote, "Had I not gone home summers and hobnobbed with folk-type Negroes, I would have finished college without knowing that any Negro other than Paul Laurence Dunbar ever wrote a poem." Among these "folk-types" he found the subjects of his earliest efforts at fiction: rustic tenants of a migrant community that he would name Mudtown, one of many such communities of blacks from the Southland. The making of Mudtown into a metaphorical scene of the African-American folk experience was enlivened by unmistakable portrayals of Grandmother Sarah Pembroke and Uncle Buddy. In upper Manhattan, in the era of the Harlem Renaissance, Arna Bontemps himself became one of those thousands of migrants to find his way to a modern metropolitan Mudtown: the Big Apple, where his hope was to write poetry and short fiction that told his people's story.

Bontemps arrived in New York City in 1924 to take a teaching post at the Harlem Academy, a predominantly black Adventist high school. This turned into a seven-year stint and represented his first sustained immersion in a black community outside of Louisiana. Within two years he met and married Alberta Johnson, an Academy student from Waycross, Georgia. The vibrant cultural atmosphere of Harlem fueled Bontemps's desire to write. Upon winning three poetry prizes in 1926 and 1927, Bontemps emerged as a New Negro poet who was to become a major literary figure in the Harlem Renaissance. His new interest in writing also resulted in the publication of *God Sends Sunday* (1931), his first published novel. *Little Augie,* the book's irrepressibly zestful central figure, was modeled after Great-uncle Buddy. Committed to his own fiction and poetry, Bontemps also devoted himself to the work of other black authors, eventually gaining respect as a prominent anthologist and folklorist. In addition to *The Book of Negro Folklore,* Bontemps and Langston Hughes edited the major anthology *The Poetry of the Negro: 1746–1949* (1949).

If Bontemps's choice of the title *God Sends Sunday* was intended to refute any association between the character portrayals and the Adventist church, it failed. Sunday Sabbaths certainly did not represent the Adventists (who worshiped on Saturdays), but the title's reference to God and the narrative's racy content were considered highly provocative by both the church and his father, who had since become an Adventist minister.

Under these heavy shadows of disapproval, Bontemps left New York with his wife and two children for a new teaching assignment at Oakwood Junior College, a segregated Adventist institution in Huntsville, Alabama, at the northern end of the state, near Tennessee.

In a 1972 interview, while recalling this move from New York to Alabama, Bontemps spoke eloquently of yearnings for an undefined something in his personal past. This first exposure to the Deep South since his Louisiana childhood seems to have been a resonant moment in Bontemps's life, a time during which longing and memory merged to awaken his senses and enliven his imagination.

The Oakwood appointment lasted three years that were intensely troubling but also extraordinarily fruitful. This period includes the publication of *Popo and Fifina: Children of Haiti* (1932), a novel for children written with Langston Hughes; Bontemps's best-known short story, "Summer Tragedy" (1932); the writing of a dozen or so other tales published posthumously in *The Old South* (1973); *You Can't Pet a Possum* (1934), a popular children's story; and the start of *Black Thunder: Gabriel's Revolt: Virginia 1800* (1936). Despite his unease with the church, Bontemps felt a personal connection with the landscape and described the Huntsville setting as "rediscovered woods and swamps and streams with which [my] ancestors had been intimate." He spoke of abounding game and hunts with dogs but without gunpowder. He spoke of spiritual people living in difficult times who made themselves ready for church when Sunday came.

Bubber Goes to Heaven emerges from just such an atmosphere. Bontemps placed the tale in the agrarian world of Huntsville by opening with a coon hunt across a verdant and darkened countryside. Bubber, an undersized adolescent, struggles to keep up. Signs indicate that this is a moment of transformation for Bubber, a rite in which man and nature conspire.

Bubber's duty to shake treed coons from their perches accounts for his ability to distinguish by name the three outstanding trees in the wood: Adam, Eve, and Nebuchadnezzar. These Old Testament markers elevate Bubber's story to the biblical plane, and Bontemps transposes the ordinary event into a spiritual one. The space in which the story takes place becomes a realm soaked in folk religion, where oral traditions prevail, and where black cultural identity is deeply embedded in the natural world.

If this is a forest of ritual, it is no accident that Bubber plunges from the branches of Nebuchadnezzar. The name refers to the ancient king and visionary creator of the famed city of Babylon and its beautiful hanging gardens. Bubber's accident takes on the quality of myth: the fall sends Bubber into a dream of heaven that sharpens his vision of an idealized place and objectifies a yearning that until now was undefined.

For Bubber, heaven is the place of his deepest longings, the dream of a "promised land" that, alas, remains unrealized. He envisions an ecumenical place where harmony prevails, where justice is secured, and where hard times are no longer among us: "I didn't see the Lawd, but I seen the square and the court house."

When Bontemps wrote this story, embattled blacks in the segregated, impoverished South were struggling to sustain just such a dream for peace and justice and were holding fast to the promise of relief. For the next four decades, Bontemps would continue to write about this black experience, often most effectively in his works for young adults. To be sure, Bontemps had begun to think of juvenile tales as more reliable moneymakers than his novels, which tended to be histories. His books for children, with their similarity to oral tale telling, provided him with a means to address the immediacy of his personal experiences. His third novel for children, *Sad-Faced Boy* (1937), proved that he would be an important children's writer. But he also produced other significant literature for young adults: in 1941 he compiled *Golden Slippers,* the first anthology of African-American poetry for children, and in 1948, he wrote the widely praised, far-ranging history *The Story of the Negro,* specifically for young people. Not only as an author but also as a teacher, lecturer, and librarian (he became librarian of Fisk University in 1943), Bontemps maintained a close connection with young blacks and continued to tell them the story—through fiction, poetry, history, and biography—of African Americans.

Arna Bontemps (1902–1973) was born in Louisiana and grew up in California. He moved to New York City in 1923, and it was there that he met Langston Hughes and other writers who were leaders of the Harlem Renaissance. Bontemps began his literary career as a poet but also wrote novels, edited anthologies of African-American poetry and folktales, and wrote many popular children's books, including *Slappy Hooper, The Fast Sooner Hound,* and *Popo and Fifina* and *The Pasteboard Bandit* (both coauthored with Hughes). Known primarily as one of our major African-American poets, Bontemps is also credited with making black folklore and literature available to the public through his anthologies and through his work as a historian, librarian, and teacher at several American universities.

Daniel Minter is originally from a small town in Georgia. He attended the Art Institute of Atlanta and received his art degree in 1981. He has been working as an artist in various media since that time. Although he considers himself a painter, he has chosen to work in the same medium as many generations of African Americans in the South, carving and painting on wood. Minter has exhibited in the United States and abroad and is currently living in Brooklyn, New York.

Jim Haskins is the author of more than 100 books for children and young adults, many of them on African-American history and culture. He is professor of English at the University of Florida and lives in Gainesville and New York City.

Charles L. James is the Sara Lawrence Lightfoot Professor and chairman of the Department of English Literature at Swarthmore College. He is editor of the critical anthology *From the Roots: Short Stories by Black Americans* and is currently writing a biography of Arna Bontemps.

Robert G. O'Meally is Zora Neale Hurston Professor of American Literature at Columbia University. He is the author of *The Craft of Ralph Ellison* and *Lady Day: Many Faces of the Lady* and editor of *Tales of the Congaree by E. C. Adams* and *New Essays on "Invisible Man."* Professor O'Meally is coeditor of *History and Memory in African-American Culture* and *Critical Essays on Sterling A. Brown.*

THE IONA AND PETER OPIE
LIBRARY OF CHILDREN'S LITERATURE

THE OPIE LIBRARY brings to a new generation an exceptional selection of children's literature, ranging from facsimiles and new editions of classic works to lost or forgotton treasures—some never before published—by eminent authors and illustrators. The series honors Iona and Peter Opie, the distinguished scholars and collectors of children's literature, continuing their lifelong mission to seek out and preserve the very best books for children.

Robert G. O'Meally, General Editor